The Ten Commandments of Grief

Table of Contents

ACKNOWLEDGMENTS	3
FIVE STAGES OF GRIEF	5
I. THE FIRST COMMANDMENT OF GRIEF **Thou Shall Not Place Other's Grief Above Yours**	15
II. THE SECOND COMMANDMENT OF GRIEF **Thou Shall Not Worship Memories Over Moving Forward**	21
III. THE THIRD COMMANDMENT OF GRIEF **Thou Shall Not Turn Away From God**	29
IV. THE FOURTH COMMANDMENT OF GRIEF **Thou Shall not neglect Thy Rest and Self-care.**	35
V. THE FIFTH COMMANDMENT OF GRIEF **Thou Shall Not Forget To Honor**	41
VI. THE SIXTH COMMANDMENT OF GRIEF **Thou Shall Not Weaponize Your Grief**	49
VII. THE SEVENTH COMMANDMENT OF GRIEF **Thou Shall Not Commit Adultery**	61
VIII. THE EIGHT COMMANDMENT OF GRIEF **Thou Shall Not Steal**	69
IX. THE NINTH COMMANDMENT OF GRIEF **Thou Shall Not Lie**	79
X. THE TENTH COMMANDMENT OF GRIEF **Thou Shall Not Covet**	87

© All rights reserved. This book or parts thereof may not be reproduced in any form, stored in any retrieval system, or transmitted in any form by any means—electronic, mechanical, photocopy, recording, or otherwise—without prior written permission of the publisher, except as provided by United States of America copyright law. For permission requests, write to the publisher, at "Attention: Permissions Coordinator," at the address below.

Published by:
Nathan E. Austin Ministries
1525 NW 7th Street
Pompano Beach FL. 33069

ACKNOWLEDGMENTS

This book is dedicated to my precious mother the late **Ruby Fryer,** whose love, wisdom, and faith laid the foundation for my journey. Your presence is forever felt, and your legacy lives on in every word of this book. Although I was not afforded the chance to say goodbye this book has helped me bring closure to the fact that you are no longer with me. To my father the late **Nathaniel Austin**. Writing this book has helped me to understand fully what grief really feels like.

To my loving and supportive wife, **Kimberly Austin,** your unwavering belief in me and your endless encouragement make all things possible.

To my dear sister, **Dr. Lynnette Austin**, and my cherished aunt, **Oscie Fryer,** your love and guidance have been a beacon in my life

To my Mother-in-Love, **Renay Davis**: Thank you for always being more than just Kim's mother. You have always been a motherly figure to me, and your presence has certainly helped fill the void left by my own mother..

To my **NEA Ministry** assistance, **Kimberly Simon** words cannot express how grateful I am to have you assist me with this project.

To my extended family in faith, the entire **Zion Church Family**, thank you for your prayers, encouragement, and support. Your love has strengthened me, and I am forever grateful.

To everyone who has supported me on this journey—thank you from the depths of my heart. Your love and encouragement inspire me daily.

With gratitude and love,

Nathan E. Austin

"Grief is the price we pay for love."

Queen Elizabeth II

"Grief is the price we pay for love." Those were the words spoken by Queen Elizabeth II as she addressed the families of the 250 British victims of the 9/11 terrorist attacks. Chances are if you are reading this you have paid or will pay that price one day. It's a price no one wants to pay. It's a price that no one thinks they can afford to pay. However when you choose to love, you involuntarily sign up to pay this price one day. Love is choice and grief is a consequence of that choice. To have never grieved is to have never loved and to have never loved is to have never lived. The moment we are given the precious gift of life is the moment we fall in love. We begin by falling in love with those who love us. Typically, those are the people we grieve the most simply because we loved them the longest.

The question that demands an answer is, what is Grief? Grief is the emotional response to a significant loss, particularly the death of a loved one. It can also stem from other types of loss, such as the end of a relationship, loss of a job, or a life-changing event.

You see, grief is not just about the loss of someone, but also the loss of something. As stated earlier, love and grief go hand in hand. My first book was entitled The 10 Commandments of Love. Never in a thousand years could I have imagined that my next book would be The 10 Commandments of Grief. However, April 10, 2024 changed my life forever. That was the day I found out that my mother had passed away unexpectedly. That was the day I hit grief head on.

I could be wrong, but love and grief are the two hallmarks of everyone's experience. I shall forever be grateful for the lives that have been touched from the 10 Commandments of Love but I am even more grateful for those who shall be comforted by reading the 10 Commandments of Grief.

If you have read or seen the title of my previous book, you may ask the question what's your infatuation with the Ten Commandments? Well I'm sure rather you practice Christianity or not, you are probably aware of the 10 Commandments found in the Holy Bible. If not, here they are:

I. *Thou shall have no other gods before Me.*
II. *Thou shall not make for yourself a carved image...*
III. *Thou shall not take the name of the LORD your God in vain...*
IV. *Remember the Sabbath day, to keep it holy.*
V. *Honor your father and your mother, that your days may be long upon the land which the LORD your God is giving you.*
VI. *Thou shall not murder.*
VII. *Thou shall not commit adultery.*
VIII. *Thou shall not steal.*
IX. *Thou shall not bear false witness against your neighbor.*
X. *Thou shall not covet your neighbor's house; you shall not covet your neighbor's wife, nor his male servant, nor his female servant, nor his ox, nor his donkey, nor anything that is your neighbor's.*

In this book we have modified the original language of the 10 Commandments to a language the connects with grief. After reading each commandment you will discover there is a section entitled "Reflections." These sections are designed for you digest and determine exactly where you are in your grief process. You will also find "Application Assignments". This is designed for you to practically apply each commandment to your everyday walk of life. I pray this book helps navigate through the never-ending journey of grief.

Let's Begin

Before we dive into the 10 Commandments of Grief I thought I would begin by sharing with you the 5 Stages of Grief. Grief is an inevitable part of the human experience, touching every life at some point. The **Five Stages of Grief**, as introduced by psychiatrist **Elisabeth Kübler-Ross** in her 1969 book *On Death and Dying*, provide a framework to understand how individuals process loss.

1. Denial – The Shock and Disbelief

"This can't be happening."

Denial is often the **first reaction** to loss. It serves as a psychological buffer, helping individuals cope with overwhelming emotions by delaying full acceptance. This stage is marked by feelings of **numbness, disbelief, and avoidance**. The mind struggles to process reality, sometimes leading to avoidance behaviors like refusing to discuss the loss or acting as if everything is normal.

Signs of Denial:

- Feeling emotionally detached or numb
- Insisting that "this isn't real"
- Avoiding reminders of the loss
- Clinging to hope that things will return to normal

The Purpose of Denial:

Denial is a defense mechanism that **protects the mind** from immediate emotional overload. It allows people to slowly absorb reality at their own pace.

2. Anger – The Search for Someone to Blame

"Why did this happen? Who is responsible?"

As reality begins to set in, pain surfaces in the form of **anger**. This anger may be directed toward oneself, others, the circumstances, or even a higher power. The unfairness of loss can make people feel **frustrated, helpless, and resentful**.

Expressions of Anger:

- Blaming doctors, family members, or even the deceased
- Feeling abandoned or betrayed
- Experiencing outbursts or irritability
- Questioning faith or life's fairness

The Purpose of Anger:

Anger is a **natural reaction** to pain and a way to externalize grief. While it may seem destructive, it can also provide a sense of control during a time of helplessness.

3. Bargaining – The "What If" and "If Only" Stage

"If only I had done something differently..."

Bargaining is an attempt to **reverse or delay** the loss. People may make silent deals with a higher power, wishing they could go back in time and change events. This stage is often filled with guilt and regret, replaying past moments to see if something could have prevented the outcome.

Common Bargaining Thoughts:

- "If I had just been there, this wouldn't have happened."
- "What if I had done more?"
- "If I promise to be a better person, can things go back to the way they were?"

The Purpose of Bargaining:

Bargaining provides **a sense of control**, even if temporary. It reflects the human desire to make sense of chaos and hold onto hope, even in situations beyond one's control.

4. Depression – The Deep Sorrow

"This loss is unbearable."

This stage brings **deep sadness, loneliness, and despair**. Unlike clinical depression, which is persistent and requires medical attention, grief-related depression is a **natural response** to loss. People in this stage may withdraw from life, struggle with motivation, or feel a deep sense of emptiness.

Signs of Grief-Related Depression:

- Feeling overwhelmed by sadness
- Losing interest in activities and relationships

- Experiencing sleep disturbances or fatigue
- Feeling as if life has lost its meaning

The Purpose of Depression:

This stage is often where people **begin to fully process their loss**. Though painful, it is a necessary step toward healing, allowing the griever to confront their emotions rather than avoid them.

5. Acceptance – Finding Peace with the Loss

"I can't change what happened, but I can learn to live with it."

Acceptance does **not mean forgetting or being okay with the loss**—it means learning to live with it. People in this stage find ways to move forward while carrying their grief. This may involve creating new routines, honoring the memory of a loved one, or finding personal growth through the experience.

What Acceptance Looks Like:
- Feeling more at peace with the loss
- Finding meaning in life despite the grief
- Reconnecting with others and engaging in life again
- Holding onto memories without them causing constant pain

The Purpose of Acceptance:

Acceptance is about **integrating grief into life**. The pain may never fully go away, but it becomes manageable, allowing individuals to move forward with hope.

While these stages do not occur in a strict order and are not experienced by everyone in the same way, they help illuminate the emotions that accompany grief. As we begin the 10 Commandments we will encounter and expand on several of these stages. Now lets explore the 10 Commandments of Grief.

Which of these stages have you experienced? Describe how it made you feel and what helped you move past it.

I

The First Commandment of Grief

Thou Shall Not Place Other's Grief Above Yours.

Exodus 20:3
"Thou shall have no other gods before Me."

Thou Shall Not Place Other's Grief Above Yours.

The First Commandment of Grief:
Thou Shall Not Place Other's Grief Above Yours.
Exodus 20:3, "Thou shall have no other gods before me"

Hello, my name is Nathan E. Austin. I have the privilege of serving as a Senior Pastor. One of the universal truths about being a Pastor is the need to put others first, even at the expense of your personal well being. I must admit, after over a decade of being a pastor, I have grown accustomed to putting my feelings and needs aside for the benefit of those I serve. The pulpit is a place of strength not weakness. Let's face it, when I stand to preach nobody really cares about what I'm going through, they just want to hear a message that will impact their lives for the better.

The truth is, it's hard always having to be the strong one. Here's the funny thing about being strong, it's exhausting! The question is why do you have to be strong? Where is it written that you must be superman or superwoman for everyone else? Where is it written that you can't make your grief about you? When you are a strong person, you are most likely the strongest in your circle. That means when death hits, everyone comes to you—and when they do, you almost always feel guilty for grieving. In times of grief, it's tempting to wear a mask, pretending to be strong for the sake of others, or even for yourself. However, true healing begins when you acknowledge your pain rather than deny it. God does not expect you to hide your sorrow; rather, He invites you to bring it to Him. Just as the first commandment reminds us to put nothing before God, the same principle applies to grief. Grief is overwhelming. When we lose someone we love, we often feel a strong responsibility to care for those who are grieving alongside us. **We want to be strong for our family, be present for our friends, and make sure everyone else is okay—even when we are falling apart inside.** While it is noble to support others in their grief, it is dangerous when we consistently prioritize their well-being at the expense of our own healing. Ignoring your own pain does not make you stronger—it only delays your ability to fully heal. If you spend all your energy making sure everyone else is okay, you may wake up one day and realize that you have completely neglected yourself.

Grief is not something that can be avoided. It demands to be felt. **When you constantly put others' needs above your own, you rob yourself of the opportunity to fully process your loss.**

Some people believe that as long as they are taking care of others, they won't have to deal with their own grief. They busy themselves with **planning funerals, comforting others, making sure their children, parents, or siblings are okay.** The truth is, grief does not disappear just because you ignore it. **It waits.** It is possible to **support others while still prioritizing your own well-being.** You cannot be strong for others if you are falling apart inside. Take time to heal, rest, and care for yourself. Your grief matters too.

Reflection:

Many people feel pressured to appear strong in grief, believing that showing pain is a sign of weakness. However, true healing begins when you allow yourself to grieve openly. God does not expect you to hide your sorrow but rather to bring it to Him.

Application Assignment:

- Write a journal entry about how you truly feel. Be honest, even if it's difficult.
- Identify one person you trust (a friend, pastor, or counselor) and have a real conversation about your grief.
- Spend time in prayer, openly expressing your sorrow to God.

II

The Second Commandment of Grief

Thou Shall Not Worship Memories Over Moving Forward.

Exodus 20:4
"Thou shall not make for yourself an idol."

Thou Shall Not Worship Memories Over Moving.

The Second Commandment of Grief
Thou Shall Not Worship Memories
Over Moving Forward.

(Exodus 20:4 - "Thou shall not make for yourself an idol.")

Cherishing memories is a natural part of grieving, but there is a fine line between honoring the past and becoming trapped in it. When memories become an idol—when they hold you captive rather than comfort you—it becomes difficult to move forward. Grief can sometimes cause people to live in the past, constantly replaying moments instead of embracing the present and the future.

The second commandment warns against making idols, and in grief, this can take the form of fixating on what was instead of what is and what can be. Some may struggle with feelings of guilt, believing that moving forward means they are forgetting their loved one. However, honoring a person's memory does not mean stopping your own life. True remembrance is found in carrying forward the lessons, love, and legacy they left behind.

Memories should be a source of comfort, not chains that bind you. When you find yourself unable to engage with the present because you are consumed by the past, it may be time to seek healing. This does not mean abandoning memories but instead learning how to integrate them in a way that brings life rather than prolongs sorrow. Creating new experiences does not dishonor the ones you have lost; rather, it is a testament to their influence in your life.

The reality is holding on too long can hinder your healing. Here are some things to consider when you are worshiping memories.

1. Emotional Paralysis – Living in the Past

Some people become so consumed by memories that they struggle to engage with life in the present. My wife and I love to watch the TV series Chicago Fire. In one of the episodes a fire fighter's injury forced him to take a early retirement with 75% pension. He was physically fit to do other things but not fit enough to be a fire fighter. After he received the news, he would come by the fire house everyday to chat it up with his former co-workers. No one thought it was strange at first, but after a while concerns started to be made. Well, one day when he came to the fire house he got missing. Two of his friends found him on the roof attempting to jump. Of course, they used their training to talk him down and while doing so they discovered that he wanted to jump because he could not imagine his life without doing the job he loved so much. He was grieving moving on! Remember, grief is all about mourning something that you've lost. He had entered a state of Emotional Paralysis. It is important that we evaluate our emotions to make sure with are not paralyzed. Here are some signs that you or someone you know may be emotionally paralyzed. Refusing to change anything in your home, keeping loved ones' belongings exactly as they left them, waking up at the same time but not doing anything, going to places without a purpose or resist creating new memories out of fear that it would be an act of betrayal. While it is natural to hold on to special mementos, there is a difference between cherishing the past and being crippled by it.

2. Preventing Others from Moving Forward

Sometimes, grief can make us unintentionally place unrealistic expectations on others. There are times when grief can create an **unspoken pressure**—a belief that no one should move forward until we feel ready ourselves. This can happen in family settings, friendships, and even in church. But true love does not imprison others in sorrow; it allows them the freedom to heal in their own way.

3. Releasing the Past Without Losing Whats In Your Heart

Letting go of **the pain of the past** is different from letting go of **what** you lost. Many people avoid moving forward because they fear they will lose their connection. Let's be honest, I know more than anyone that there are some once in a lifetime connections we all make. Nothing or no one will ever come close to those connections. (I'll discuss later in the book how to lean on suitable substitutes) However in reality, the **love, wisdom, and impact** of what you lost will never leave us. The goal of grief is not to forget but to reach a place where remembering them brings peace instead of only pain.

4. Not Trusting God's Plan for the Future

Ecclesiastes 3:1 reminds us, *"For everything there is a season, a time for every purpose under heaven."* This includes a **time to mourn** but also a **time to heal**. God does not ask us to erase the past, but He does call us to **walk into the future with hope**.

When we hold too tightly to the past, we may miss the blessings God still has in store. There is still purpose for your life beyond grief. There are people who still need the best version of YOU! Your story is not over because of loss—God can bring something beautiful even out of sorrow.

God desires that you continue living with purpose. Jeremiah 29:11 reminds us that He has plans for us, even after deep loss. Though the pain of absence is real, the presence of God is even greater. Trust that He will guide you through grief into a place where memories bring joy instead of just sadness.

If you find yourself stuck in a cycle of reliving the past, consider finding new ways to honor your loved one.

Application Assignments:

1. **Write a Gratitude Letter** – Instead of focusing only on loss, write a letter to your loved one expressing gratitude for the time you had with them.

2. **Create a New Memory in Their Honor** – Do something meaningful in their memory that brings joy and healing. **(I started a Facebook group entitled MAMA LOOK. It's a place where people can update their loved ones about special events and accomplishments they missed because**

they are gone.) *Click our QR Code to join this group.*

3. **Release an Item That Keeps You Stuck** – If you have held onto something out of guilt rather than love, consider releasing it in a way that brings peace.

III

The Third Commandment of Grief

Thou Shall Not Turn Away From God.

Exodus 20:7
"Thou shall not misuse the name of the Lord."

Thou Shall Not Turn Away From God.

The Third Commandment of Grief
Thou Shall Not Turn Away From God.
(Exodus 20:7 - "Thou shall not misuse the name of the Lord.")

As a minister of the Gospel and a lover of our Lord and Savior Jesus Christ, I can truly say that Grief can shake the very foundation of your faith. Many people in their sorrow find themselves questioning God's goodness, His love, and even His existence. It is natural to wrestle with these thoughts. However, allowing grief to drive you away from God rather than toward Him can lead to bitterness and despair. The enemy often uses grief as an opportunity to plant seeds of doubt, causing people to feel abandoned and alone.

The third commandment warns against misusing God's name. In grief, this can manifest as blaming God for loss or turning away from Him in anger. While it is okay to bring your honest emotions before God, we must make sure that in doing so we do not harden our heart against Him. Some people stop praying, stop attending church, and even reject faith altogether because they cannot reconcile their loss with God's love.

A lot of our anger with God is attached to the bargaining stage of grief. I once met a woman in Gainesville, FL. by the name of Rachel Freeman. I was there on a preaching assignment and afterwards I was selling and signing my first book "The 10 Commandments of Love. The message I preached was entitled "So Much To Be Thankful For. It was the Sunday before Thanksgiving 2024. I mentioned how if I was honest, I wasn't looking forward to celebrating Thanksgiving because it would be the first one without my mother. I expressed my frustration and the anger I had towards God. I was angry not because he took her, but the manner in which he took her. I remember vividly Ms. Freeman standing in the line telling me she did not have money for my book, but she wanted to share something with me. Well, my first thought was "if you don't have any money, move out of the way for the paying customers". Haha! However the spirit told me to let her talk. She begin to tell me, how she truly understood my pain. "I prayed, I believed, I did everything right—and God still took my loved one". She was transparent by telling me that her grief turned into resentment, and she stopped talking to God altogether. Yet over time, she realized that turning away from God wasn't bringing her peace—it was deepening her pain. Slowly, she began to pray again, come to church again and now she is back in love with God again! She learned that faith isn't about understanding everything; it's about trusting God even in the unknown. By the way, I blessed her with my book because she didn't realize how much I needed to hear that that day. Even when we're upset with God, He has a unique way of giving us exactly what we need, right when we need it most.

When grief tempts you to walk away from your faith, remember that God's love is not defined by circumstances. The presence of pain does not mean the absence of God. Instead of shutting Him out, invite Him into your grief. Allow Him to carry you through the darkness, even when you do not understand His plan.

It is okay to have questions. It is okay to not have all the answers. But in your grief, do not let the enemy convince you that God is against you. He is for you, with you, and able to bring beauty out of ashes. Hold onto your faith, even when it is small, and let God lead you to healing.

Reflection:
It is normal to wrestle with your faith after loss, but turning away from God in anger can leave you feeling even more lost. He welcomes your honest questions and is present even in your pain.

Application Assignment:
- Read Job 38:1–15, 39–41. These scriptures unpack Job's questions for God after losing everything he loved so dearly. Meditate on how God reminds us that His grace is sufficient.

- Write down any frustrations or doubts you have toward God. Pray over them, asking Him to reveal His presence to you.

- Attend a church service, Bible study, or listen to worship music as a way to reconnect spiritually.

IV

The Fourth Commandment of Grief

Thou Shall Not Neglect Thy Rest and Self-care.

Exodus 20:8
"Remember the Sabbath day by keeping it holy."

Thou Shall Not Neglect Thy Rest and Self-care.

The Fourth Commandment of Grief
Thou Shall Not Neglect Thy Rest and Self-care.
(Exodus 20:8 - "Remember the Sabbath day by keeping it holy.")

Grief is not only emotional; it takes a physical toll on the body. For many people, grief places us in GO MODE! I remember coming home from Orlando after my mother passed. It was in the wee hours of the morning. All I can remember is standing in my living room crying on my wife's shoulder and in mid cry saying "what time do we meet with the funeral home." From that moment, I was on the go for two straight weeks. The strange thing about it was, April had already been set aside as my Sabbath Month. I was not scheduled to preach or teach for the entire month. The Sunday after my mom's funeral I remember sitting in Twin Peaks restaurant talking to my friend Pastor C. Porter who had flown in to preach for us. He asked me when was I planning to return back to preaching. My immediate response was 1st Sunday. He and my wife laughed and said "you do realize that 1st Sunday is next Sunday". Of course I had no idea. My default response was from my previous prearranged schedule. (returning back in May) I never took into account that I was not ready, heck I hadn't even been studying. I was thinking like a robot and not as a real person.

Many people, overwhelmed by sorrow, neglect their own well-being. They lose sleep, skip meals, withdraw from the very things that could help them heal or jump back into their old normal to soon. While grief is exhausting, failing to care for yourself only makes the journey harder. Just as God commanded rest on the Sabbath, grieving hearts must also take time to rest and restore. My church found out my crazy idea about returning back to preach and they blocked it at every turn. They demanded that I take another 4 weeks to grieve and heal. In hindsight I can truly say, if I had not taken that time off I properly would not be alive today.

When grief comes, it is easy to ignore your body's needs. Sleep often feels impossible, eating may seem pointless, and simple activities like showering or walking outside feel overwhelming. However, failing to take care of yourself only deepens the pain. God designed the Sabbath as a day of rest because He knew that our bodies and minds need renewal. If you are grieving, make rest a priority. Even if sleep is difficult, find moments to pause, breathe, and allow yourself to relax.

You may not have the ability to take as much time off as I did but be intentional. Grieving hearts need **intentional time** to pause, process, and restore their strength.

Taking care of yourself while grieving is not a luxury; it is a necessity. Rest is not an escape from grief—it is an essential part of healing. Self-care does not mean selfishness. It is an act of survival. Nourish your body with healthy food, go for walks, and find small moments of joy where you can. Even Jesus, in His time of sorrow, withdrew to rest and pray. Taking care of yourself is not a betrayal of your loved one—it is an act of honoring the life they would want you to live.

If grief has left you feeling drained, take this as a reminder: You are allowed to rest. You are allowed to heal. You are allowed to find peace in the midst of sorrow. Trust that God is walking with you, and allow yourself the grace to recover, one step at a time.

Reflection:

Grief takes a physical toll on your body. Ignoring your needs—whether sleep, nutrition, or relaxation—only prolongs your suffering. Rest is not a sign of giving up but of honoring your body and spirit.

Application Assignment:

- Set a bedtime routine that allows for rest. Avoid distractions that interfere with sleep.

- Plan one self-care activity this week, such as taking a walk, reading, catch up on some tv shows find a new movie on Netflix, engage in a hobby.

- Make sure you are drinking water and eating healthy meals.

V

The Fifth Commandment of Grief

Thou Shall Not Forget to Honor

Exodus 20:12

"Honor your father and mother."

Thou Shall Not Forget to Honor.

The Fifth Commandment of Grief
Thou Shall Not Forget to Honor.
(Exodus 20:12 - "Honor your father and mother.")

Too often, grief becomes so consuming that people focus only on their pain rather than the legacy left behind by their loved ones. Likewise, in the midst of our sorrow, we may take for granted the **people who supported us**—friends, family, pastors, and even strangers who showed up during our time of need. True honor involves both remembering those who have passed **and** expressing gratitude to those who have stood beside us. Just as the commandment to honor parents involves **love, respect, and connection**, grief should lead us to honor the relationships in our lives—both past and present.

Honor means remembering. It means keeping the memory of our loved one alive while also acknowledging those who continue to be present for us. As we have already mentioned, to only honor the dead is to border on the lines of idolatry.

Let me share the full story of my mother's passing. I am blessed to be the Multimedia Director for the Florida General Baptist Convention. The week of her passing, I was in Orlando when I received a phone call from my wife, who told me that neither she nor my aunt had heard from my mother that day. She proceeded to tell me she was about to drive over to my mother's house to make sure that she was OK. Unfortunately, she found my mother had passed away in her sleep. I'll never fully understand the feeling my wife had at that moment as our two sons were in the car with her at the time. She was forced to compose herself for their sake all while trying to figure out how to tell me the heartbreaking news. She knew that I was in the middle of a major production as the President of the Convention was giving his 1st Annual Address as State President. There were hundreds of people in the room and thousands watching online; all of which I was fully responsible for. Instead of calling me back directly, she contacted a Pastor friend of mine Pastor Ken Johnson who then reached out to Pastor Al Jackson Jr. and Rev. Johnny Barber who were also there at the convention to help give me the news of my mother's passing. Deep down in my heart I knew something was not right, I think long before that came to see me, I had already processed what had happened. Nevertheless, when I saw them approaching me I had already started to break down because I knew what they were about to say.

Once they officially told me that my worst fears had come true, my first though was "I have to get home NOW! Keep in mind I'm in charge of all of the audio and video equipment at the convention. It's over 50 thousand dollars' worth of speakers, cameras and media equipment. Not to mention the convention was not over which means I can't break everything down nor can I leave it all behind. I had to rely on my partner brother Alex to facilitate the rest of the conference. Since we only had one more light day left, we came up with a plan to break down the equipment we no longer needed. All the pastors I mentioned without hesitation started assisting me with breaking down the equipment so I wouldn't have to do it all by himself. At this time, it's around 10:00 PM. We spent the next two to three hours breaking down equipment and talking about all types of things. We all served together at the same church so we have 20 years of history to talk about which helped pass the time. As we were close to finishing it dawned on me "what am I going to do now? It's 1:00 AM, I'm tired but I need to get home. Nobody there or my wife at home wanted me to hit the road by myself, but what choice do I have. Well thankfully my wife came up with a plan. We have two good friends of ours (Artise and Farrah Stanley) who happened to live in the Orlando area. Unbeknownst to me my wife called them and asked if they would help me to travel back to Miami. At 1:00 AM they left their homes and met me at the hotel. When they arrived, Artise jumped in my car while Farrah trailed us and drove me 90 mins to the Turnpike Plaza in Fort Pierce FL. My wife, our friend Adriana and my Executive Pastor Brandon came from Miami to meet us at the Plaza. My Executive Pastor jumped in my car and continued to drive me home while the Stanleys headed back to Orlando. We arrived back in South Florida around 4:00 AM. I know that's a lot! All the parties involved had just worked a full day and had to go to work the next day, however they did not think twice about helping me get home. I'm not sure if I'm writing this book if they had not done what they did. Driving three hours alone—in shock, disbelief, and anger—would not have been healthy for me, and my friends and family knew it. Thankfully, I didn't have to. I was not alone.

One of the best things about my process was I had a major support group. The hundreds of people who called, text, e-mailed, inboxed, along with amazing people I pastor at The Zion Church helped me go through this process. I shared all of this so you can get a full picture of what support looks like. I'm sure you've had a similar support system in your time of grieving. That's why this commandment is so important. Honor must go beyond the person or thing you lost. We must also honor those that helped us grieve. By honoring those who helped you grieve you are indeed keeping those precious memories alive.

Here are some simple ways you can maintain honor for those who helped you grieve.

Say Thank You – A simple note, call, or heartfelt conversation can mean the world to someone who supported you. You will never know what a person sacrificed to be their for you.
Spend Time with Those Who Stood by You – Grief makes time feel like it stands still, but your relationships still need care.
Pay It Forward – Honor those who helped you by being there for others in need. Once you know that value of support you should strive to be a support system for someone else.
Share Gratitude Publicly – Whether in church, social media, work or community gatherings, recognize the people who helped carry your burden.
Pray for Them – Cover the ones who helped you in prayer, asking God to bless them as they have blessed you.

Reflection:
Honoring is an **act of love**, and love is stronger than death. Even though someone is no longer physically present, their **impact continues** through the way we live, remember, and give thanks.

- Honor your loved one by living a life that reflects their best qualities.
- Honor those who helped you by expressing your gratitude.
- Honor God by trusting Him with your grief and your future.

Application Assignment:

- How can I keep my loved one's legacy alive in a way that brings healing?
- Have I taken time to appreciate those who stood by me in my grief?
- What is one step I can take today to honor someone special?

_____
_____
_____
_____
_____
_____
_____
_____
_____
_____
_____
_____
_____
_____

VI

The Sixth Commandment of Grief

Thou Shall Not Weaponize Your Grief

Exodus 20:13
"Thou shall not murder."

Thou Shall Not Weaponize Your Grief.

The Sixth Commandment of Grief: Thou Shall Not Weaponize Your Grief.
(Exodus 20:13 - "Thou shall not murder.")

Grief is one of the most powerful emotions a person can experience. It can **break you or build you, draw you closer to others or push them away, bring healing or cause destruction.** How we handle grief not only affects us—it affects those around us. When grief is **not processed in a healthy way,** it can turn into a weapon, inflicting harm on ourselves and others.

The sixth commandment says, *"You shall not murder,"* but **not all harm is physical.** Words, actions, and even silence can wound those we love. Some lash out in anger, pushing away the very people who want to help. Others internalize their pain, letting it eat away at them until they are drowning in sorrow. Some use their grief to manipulate or guilt-trip others, making them feel responsible for their suffering. And some, fueled by loss and injustice, allow grief to **turn into vengeance**, seeking to punish those they believe contributed to their pain.

Grief does not give us a license to be reckless with our emotions or relationships. **It is not an excuse to mistreat those around us, destroy ourselves, or seek revenge.** Pain is real, but it does not have to be a weapon. Grief, when not handled with care, can **destroy** even the strongest relationships. **What should be a season of leaning on others can turn into a season of isolation and brokenness.**

When Grief Becomes a Weapon of Revenge

One of the most dangerous ways grief can be weaponized is through **revenge**. When a person experiences a loss that feels unfair, unjust, or caused by another, it is easy to allow anger to take over. Revenge may not always look like physical violence—it can be emotional, social, or spiritual retaliation against someone we hold responsible for our pain.

Some people use their grief as a means to destroy reputations, sever relationships, or make others suffer because they are suffering. They allow bitterness to take root, feeding their pain with a desire to see others hurt as much as they do. As a Pastor I'm all to familiar with seeing weaponized grief. I've come to the conclusion that a lot of it stems from a person's guilt.

Guilt is a heavy and complex emotion often intertwined with grief. It's common to feel not only sadness but also regret, blame, and guilt following a loss. Two particularly challenging forms of guilt grief are:

- **The guilt of feeling you did not do enough or weren't there enough for the person you've lost.**
- **The guilt experienced when you feel directly or indirectly responsible for someone's death or loss.**

Both forms can deeply impact your emotional health, your relationships, and your path to healing. Lets explore both of these forms.

#1 Guilt for Not Doing or Being Enough

This type of guilt grief arises when someone believes they failed to adequately care for, spend time with, or express love to their loved one before their passing. People often reflect on opportunities missed, conversations not had, and gestures of love left unspoken. As I stated I was in Orlando when my mother passed. I left out on a Sunday. The previous day my wife had a First Lady's brunch in which my mom was in attendance. She was happy, smiling, dancing and taking tons of pictures. I remember saying to her, "you are having a great time today." Later that day I went over to her house to bring her groceries and to make sure her water tank was filled since I knew I would be gone for the week. As her only child these were my responsibilities to her. As I was leaving I gave her a hug and said "see you when I get back". I texted her later that day to tell her that I made it. We didn't talk much that week because my days and nights were hectic. She texted me mid-week asking when was I coming home. I told her Friday. She passed on Thursday. Although I was there for my mom, something in me still feels guilty about not communicating more with her that week. I feel that if I had talked with her on Wednesday, I could have sensed something was wrong and maybe could have done something about it.

These are some of the thoughts I still wrestle with.

- *"If only I had spent more time with her."*
- *"I should have called more."*
- *"I never told him her much I really loved her."*

Though common, guilt can lead to deep regret, emotional isolation, and depression. Left unresolved, it can consume one's life, creating emotional paralysis and prevent healing.

The truth is, when I talk to others about this I've discovered that almost everyone experiences this type of regret after losing someone they love. Life's imperfections often become magnified through grief, making normal human actions or oversights seem unforgivable. God, however, never expects perfection from us—only genuine love and honest effort. Understanding this truth can help release you from the emotional prison created by self-imposed guilt and stop you from using it as a weapon.

2 Guilt for Being Responsible for Someone's Death or Loss

Perhaps even more complex is the grief experienced by someone who carries responsibility—real or perceived—for the loss. This might be the guilt felt by the driver who caused an accident, a caretaker whose loved one passed away under their supervision, or even a parent whose child tragically died under circumstances they feel they could have prevented.

This type of guilt grief often leads to overwhelming shame, deep self-blame, and sometimes even a sense of unworthiness to continue living a normal, joyful life. It may sound like:

- *"It's my fault they're gone."*
- *"They would still be here if I hadn't made that decision."*
- *"I don't deserve forgiveness or peace."*

People burdened by such guilt often punish themselves emotionally or physically, withdrawing from relationships, joy, and faith. It's a grief that becomes self-destructive, making it feel impossible to move forward.

I would like to add a solution to help with this type of guilt.

How to Treat A Person who is Responsible for a Death or Loss.
In the movie "The Forge," Joshua Moore faces the profound tragedy of losing his 17-year-old son, Jalen, to a drunk driving accident. Initially, Joshua is consumed by anger and a desire for vengeance toward the man responsible for his son's death. However, through his faith and mentorship from an elder in his church, Joshua undergoes a transformative journey, leading him to forgive the drunk driver. Remarkably, Joshua extends grace by mentoring the very individual who caused his unimaginable loss, embodying the film's powerful theme of forgiveness and redemption. This is the perfect picture of "Forgiveness".

Even in this most painful form of grief, God offers hope. Scripture reminds us repeatedly of the possibility and necessity of forgiveness—not just from God but also from oneself. Romans 8:1 says, *"Therefore, there is now no condemnation for those who are in Christ Jesus."* Forgiveness is difficult, especially forgiving oneself, but it is also essential to true healing. I often remind my church that forgiveness is never for the other person, forgiveness is for you; even when you are the one who needs forgiving. In this instance forgiveness helped both parties.

When Silence Becomes a Weapon in Grief

Grief has many expressions—tears, anger, questions, even numbness—but perhaps one of the most harmful and misunderstood expressions is **silence**. Silence, though often perceived as harmless or neutral, can become a subtle yet devastating weapon in relationships affected by grief. You can kill a relationship without saying one word.

At times, people who grieve choose silence because they feel misunderstood or overwhelmed. They might think it's easier to remain quiet rather than burden others with their feelings. However, when silence is used as a shield or as a form of withdrawal, it becomes destructive. It creates barriers, drives wedges between family members, friends, and spouses, and isolates the grieving person from the very sources of comfort and healing they desperately need.

Consider the parent who loses a child and responds with prolonged silence toward the remaining family members. They may avoid conversation altogether, retreating into a world of solitude and pain. This silence can speak louder than words, communicating rejection, blame, or resentment—even when such feelings aren't intended. Loved ones around them may interpret the silence as personal rejection, believing they've somehow failed or caused offense. Slowly but surely, relationships weaken and can even collapse under the weight of what remains unsaid.

Sometimes, silence becomes a weapon of punishment or revenge. A grieving spouse might refuse to communicate, withholding conversation and affection as a form of emotional retaliation. Without realizing it, their grief-driven silence becomes a source of harm, causing deep emotional wounds that can outlast the original pain of the loss.

Silence doesn't only harm relationships—it also hurts the individual who employs it. When grief remains locked inside, unexpressed and unprocessed, it can lead to emotional breakdowns, anxiety, depression, and severe loneliness. Silence might initially feel protective, but over time it becomes a prison that traps the griever inside their pain.

The Bible teaches us about the power and necessity of communication in our pain. Job, suffering greatly, voiced his grief openly. The Psalms overflow with heartfelt expressions of pain, confusion, and sorrow. Jesus himself spoke openly to His disciples about His grief and anguish in the Garden of Gethsemane (Matthew

26:36-39). None of these expressions indicate weakness; rather, they reveal authenticity and provide a healthy path toward healing.

Breaking silence isn't easy, but it's essential for healing. Communication builds bridges; silence builds walls. Choosing to share our grief with others—trusted friends, family, counselors, or even in prayer—helps us process pain constructively. It invites support, compassion, and understanding rather than isolation and misunderstanding.

Ultimately, silence is not always golden. When grief is concerned, silence can become a dangerous weapon—one that harms rather than heals. Choose instead to voice your pain, share your burden, and let others walk alongside you. The journey through grief is too difficult to walk alone, and there is strength in breaking the silence. So when grief has arrested you, you DO NOT have the right to remain silence. Anything you say can and will be used as a tool to build unity. While silence can destroy, your expressions can be used to bring **healing, strength, and purpose.** When we allow grief to work **for us** rather than against us, it becomes a force that uplifts, inspires, and changes lives instead of destroying them.

As I bring this chapter to a close, I'd like to share a funny story. Just a few days after my mom's passing, my son had a field day at school." Although I wasn't feeling up to it, I went to participate because I wanted to make sure he was happy. I knew that my presence would do us both some good, especially since he was also grieving the loss of his G-Mama. We began to play a kickball game; I was in the field and the student kicked the ball to me. Immediately when I retrieved the ball I could feel the anger and frustration all over me as I was thinking about my mother's death. I knew in that moment that if I threw the ball at the child I would have thrown it with so much force that it would have probably cause some physical damage. I decided instead of throwing the ball, to run and tap the student so they could be out. "Well, the funny thing is, I'm not as young as I used to be. I ran full speed, which wasn't a problem — the problem was I couldn't stop." As a result, I ran face forward into a metal gate. I've included a picture of my gash above my eye which required several stitches. I must admit at that moment I wanted to weaponize my grief when I had the ball in my hand. Although I didn't, the thought of me doing so caused me personal harm. This is why it's important not to weaponize our grief.

Ps. Please don't laugh at my pain, enough of my friends have done so already!!!

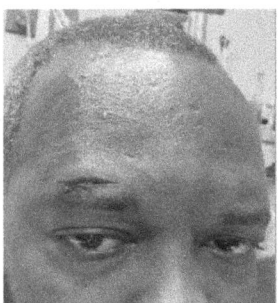

Reflection:

Guilt grief, whether it arises from perceived shortcomings or actual responsibility, is burdensome—but not beyond God's healing. Grief should never be used a weapon to hurt but an opportunity to heal.

Application Assignment:
- Instead of withdrawing, be honest. Tell people, "I'm struggling, but I still need you."
- Call someone you may be estranged from because of grief. Make an effort to restore the relationship.
- Instead of assuming others don't care, recognize, "They might not know what to say, but that doesn't mean they don't love me."

_____
_____
_____
_____
_____
_____

VII

The Seventh Commandment of Grief

Thou Shall Not Use Grief to Commit Adultery

Exodus 20:14 -
"Thou shall not commit adultery."

Thou Shall Not Use Grief to Commit Adultery.

The Seventh Commandment of Grief
Thou Shall Not Use Grief to Commit Adultery.
(Exodus 20:14 - "Thou shall not commit adultery.")

Grief, in its deepest moments, makes a person vulnerable. It creates an emptiness that longs to be filled, a pain that seeks comfort, and a loneliness that yearns for companionship. In that longing, some turn to **adultery**. Adultery is often thought of as simply being unfaithful in marriage, but in the context of grief, it can mean much more. It can mean **betraying your values, compromising your integrity, and abandoning your own future** because sorrow clouds your judgment. Some people cheat on their spouse with another person, seeking solace in the arms of someone else to numb the pain. Others cheat themselves out of their own destiny, abandoning their dreams, goals, and the life they were meant to live because they no longer see the point.

Grief and the Temptation to Find Healing in the Wrong Arms

Losing a loved one leaves a void. When a spouse dies, that void is filled with silence, loneliness, and aching memories of what was. When a child is lost, the emptiness can be unbearable. When a close friend or family member is taken away, the comfort of their presence is no longer there to support you. In this state of vulnerability, some seek healing in ways that are destructive—through affairs, unhealthy relationships, additions, or reckless emotional connections that **do not heal but instead deepen the wound.**

Many who have lost a significant other rush into relationships too soon, **not out of love, but out of desperation to ease the pain.** They mistake attraction for healing, seeking someone to replace what was lost rather than truly allowing themselves time to heal. I hate the fact that I've personally witnessed marriages torn apart after the loss of a child. When couples go through something traumatic only two things will happen. They will build a stronger bond, or they will be driven apart. There's no in between. I'm inspired by the passage of scripture found in *Job 42:12 the Lord blessed the latter part of Job's life more than the former part. He had fourteen thousand sheep, six thousand camels, a thousand yoke of oxen and a thousand donkeys. ¹³ And he also had seven sons and three daughters.* What's special about this scripture is that in Job chapter 1 Job and his wife lost all 10 of their children, However by the end of the book they had come together to have 10 more children. I'm sure a lot of tears were shed during this process, but the good news is they were able to bounce back together as a couple. Grief did Not WIN!

Grief makes people crave connection, but **not all connections are meant to be made in moments of weakness.** Love born out of pain rather than healing often leads to more brokenness. Instead of seeking people to **numb the pain**, grief must be processed in a way that allows real healing to take place.

I could easily expand on Adultery in the most familiar sense but you can read Commandment 7 in my Previous Book "The 10 Commandments of Love". There I dive deeper into the matter.

Grief as a Form of Adultery Against Yourself

Beyond unfaithfulness in a relationship, grief can lead to **adultery against yourself**—a betrayal of the future God has for you. Some people cheat on themselves by **giving up on their dreams, abandoning their purpose, and choosing to exist rather than to live.**

When someone is grieving, they may believe that life no longer holds meaning. They may stop pursuing the dreams they once had, put aside their ambitions, and let their grief dictate the rest of their life. A person who losses someone can abandon their career and passions, believing that nothing matters anymore. They stop taking care of their self, opportunities pass them by, and they lose sight of the dreams they once had.

This kind of grief-driven **self-betrayal** is its own form of adultery. It is **a betrayal of your own potential, your own future, and the life you were meant to live.** You were not created to remain stuck in sorrow. Though grief is a natural process, it is **not the end of your story.** When grief tempts you to give up on your own story, remember that God is not done with you. Choosing to press forward does not mean you forget what you lost—it means you honor by continuing to live.

Reflection:

Adultery is not just about being unfaithful to a spouse—it is about being unfaithful to **yourself, your future, and the healing process that God wants for you.** If grief has tempted you to seek comfort in the wrong places or to abandon the dreams you once had, know that it is **not too late to turn back.**

You were not meant to **stop living** because of grief. You were not meant to **abandon your calling** because of sorrow. And you were not meant to **seek healing in places that will only bring more pain.**

Application Assignment:

Healing Without Betraying Yourself or Others

So how do you grieve without **cheating yourself, your loved ones, or your future?**

- **Allow yourself time to heal before rushing into new relationships.** Love is a beautiful thing, but love born from **pain rather than wholeness** often leads to more heartbreak.

- **Do not abandon your calling.** The person you lost would not want you to stop living. Honor them by continuing to grow, dream, and pursue the future.

- **Seek comfort in God before seeking it in temporary fixes.** The pain is real, but God is a healer. When you place your grief in His hands, He leads you to true restoration rather than quick solutions.

- **Who or what** have you **abandoned or betrayed** because of grief?

VIII

The Eighth Commandment of Grief

Thou Shall Not Steal

Exodus 20:15 -

"Thou shall not steal."

"The thief comes only to steal and kill and destroy; I have come that they may have life, and have it to the full." (John 10:10)

Thou Shall Not Steal.

The Eighth Commandment of Grief
Thou Shall Not Steal.
Exodus 20:15 - "Thou shall not steal.")

"The thief comes only to steal and kill and destroy; I have come that they may have life, and have it to the full." (John 10:10)

When we think about stealing, we often picture someone taking money, possessions, or opportunities that don't belong to them. But stealing is not just about physical things—it's about **taking something that was never meant to be yours.**

Grief, when left unchecked, can become a thief. It can **steal your joy, your peace, your faith, your purpose, and your relationships.** Even worse, grief can cause you to **steal things that don't belong to you—such as depression, laziness, withdrawal, and a false sense of control.** These burdens were never meant for you to carry, but grief can trick you into picking them up and keeping them as your own.

Stealing is not always intentional. Sometimes, it happens slowly, without realizing it. One day, you are simply mourning, and the next, you find that grief has stolen years of your life. It is crucial to recognize when grief is robbing you and when you are **holding on to things that were never meant for you.**

Grief Can Steal What God Intended for You

When grief is not handled with care, it has the power to take away the very things God still wants you to have. Here are some of the most common things grief can steal:

1. Grief Can Steal Your Joy

Losing someone you love can make happiness feel impossible. Even moments of laughter can feel wrong, as though enjoying life is a betrayal of the one who has passed. You may feel guilty when you smile or when you find peace in the midst of sorrow. But this is how grief steals joy—by convincing you that **happiness is no longer allowed.** Joy is not a betrayal—it is a gift from God. **Grief may last for a season, but it should not steal joy forever.** *Weeping may endure for a night, but joy comes in the morning."* (Psalm 30:5) I've learned that grief has a profound impact on a person's emotions, motivation, and overall well-being, no matter what your status in life is. Anybody who knows me knows that I'm a huge Miami Heat fan. (my mother was as well) In January of 2025, one the stars of the team (Jimmy Butler) came out and made a statement that he had lost his Joy! To give you a little context Jimmy wanted the team to extend his contract for a few more years. The Heat were unwilling to agree to the terms that Jimmy desired. Not long after their decision, Jimmy made this statement. It would be easy to assume that the statement was made because Jimmy simply wanted more money. However, I want to peel the onion back a little. Those who have been close to the Heat can admit Jimmy had not been his self for quite some time. Well, what most may not know is that Jimmy lost his father after a long illness in February of 2024. Can we speculate that this too could be a contributing factor of Jimmy's change of behavior. For Butler, basketball has been a major part of his identity and life journey, but grief can make even a lifelong passion feel hollow. It's common for people dealing with loss to struggle with focus, motivation, and emotional energy—things that are essential for a high-level athlete. His public statements about losing joy could have been more than just contract negotiations; they could reflect a deeper emotional battle that many people go through when dealing with the death of a loved one.

In sports, athletes are often expected to perform at a high level no matter what personal struggles they face. But grief doesn't follow a set timeline, and it can manifest in different ways—mental fatigue, a lack of motivation, or even a reevaluation of life goals. Butler might be questioning what truly matters to him, leading to uncertainty about his future in the game.

Of course, contract negotiations are always a factor in professional sports, but it's important not to overlook the human side of the story. Butler's emotions may be intertwined with his grief, making it hard to separate business decisions from personal struggles. If his joy for the game is fading, it might not just be about money—it could be about finding meaning and purpose after a significant personal loss. For Butler, a change of scenery could be the very thing he needs to get his joy back. (Of course, a few extra million always helps!)

The opposite of joy is sadness. However the extreme opposite of joy is anger. It's important to monitor your anger when you are grieving. The least little thing can set you off. When my mother passed, I remember telling my wife that I was not in a position to discipline our children for a while because I did not trust my actions. (To be honest I still wrestle with those feelings). A simple disciplinary conversation could easily turn into something worst. Grief had taken my joy.

2. Grief Can Steal Your Peace

One of the first ways grief robs you of peace is by planting the seed of **regret**. After a loss, the mind begins replaying **all the things you should have done differently.** The weight of these thoughts can be **overwhelming, suffocating, and exhausting.** The enemy uses these "what ifs" to put you back into a cycle of guilt, convincing you that you could have prevented the loss. But this is a lie. My prayer for you is that God will give you peace in the midst of your storm of grief.

3. Grief Steals Your Rest

Grief often makes it difficult to **sleep, focus, and function.** The mind becomes overactive, racing with thoughts, memories, and emotions that **won't let you rest.** When you are grieving you must monitor:

- **Sleepless Nights:** Many grieving people lie awake at night, unable to find peace, tormented by memories and sorrow. I have lost count of the amount of times I prayed that my mother would visit me in my sleep.

- **Physical Fatigue:** Lack of sleep turns into **exhaustion, headaches, and even illness.** When you are physically fatigue no amount of coffee, B-12 or Red Bull will compensate for rest. God created our bodies to restore itself, and the way we do that is through rest. If we allow grief to steal our rest, we will always feel tired.

- **Mental Fog:** Without proper rest, it becomes difficult to think clearly, make decisions, or fully engage with life. I've personally noticed that I haven't been as sharp as I once was. For a while, I attributed it to age, but it wasn't until recently that I realized a lack of real rest was the biggest contributing factor to my mental fogGod does not want you to carry your grief alone. **He offers rest, but you must be willing to receive it.** *Come to me, all who are weary and burdened, and I will give you rest."* (Matthew 11:28)

Do Not Steal What Was Never Meant for You to Carry

1. Depression

Depression is not the same as grief. Grief is a process; depression is **a deep emotional weight that keeps you stuck.** When you refuse to heal, you **take on** something that was never meant for you. God does not want you to live in **permanent sorrow.** You can grieve and still move forward in **hope.**

2. Control

There's no doubt grief makes everything seem out of control. Some people, after experiencing a loss, try to **take control of everything** around them to prevent further pain. **Control is an illusion.** No amount of planning can prevent future pain. The only true peace comes from surrendering your **life, your loved ones, and your future to God.** Remember God has and will always be in control over every situation, even your GRIEF!

**Whatever Grief Has Caused You to Steal,
It's Time to Give It Back**

Reflection:

Grief may have stolen something from you, but it **does not have to keep it.**

Application Assignment:

Have you allowed grief to steal your joy? It's time to give it back to God and reclaim your ability to smile, laugh, and experience life again.

Has grief stolen your purpose? It's time to return to the dreams and callings God placed in your heart, knowing that your future still matters.

Did grief steal your relationships? If you have pushed people away, now is the time to let them back in. Rebuild the connections that grief tried to destroy.

Has grief stolen your peace? If your mind has been filled with regret, fear, or sleepless nights, surrender them to God and let His peace replace them.

The enemy wants grief to **hold you hostage,** but God wants to set you **free.** You don't have to let sorrow steal another moment of your life.

IX

The Ninth Commandment of Grief

Thou Shall Not Lie.

Exodus 20:16
"Thou shall not give false testimony."

Thou Shall Not Lie.

The Ninth Commandment of Grief
Thou Shall Not Lie.
Exodus 20:16 - "Thou shall not give false testimony.")

To solidify this commandment, let me be totally transparent: I've been guilty of breaking every single one of these commandments. And this one is probably the one I've broken the most. I've spent most of the book talking about the passing of my mother. However, in 2016 I lost my father to cancer. Unlike my mother's death my father's death was slow and painful to watch. All my life he was a larger than life figure, I had never seem him in pain or even sleep for that matter. To watch him suffer was not something I enjoyed.

One of the biggest dangers in grief is pretending to be okay when you are not. Society often makes people feel that they must "be strong" or "keep it together" for the sake of others. As a result, many people put on a brave face, telling others (and themselves) that they are fine when they are still deeply hurting. But lying to yourself about your grief only delays the healing process.

We've talked about the 2 months I took off after my mom's passing but for my father it was just the opposite. We had his funeral on Saturday, and I preached the next day. I took no time off. I hid behind the mask of expectation and strength. Because I was expecting him to pass, I convinced others and myself that I had the strength to withstand it. At the repast, I shook hands, smiled, and told everyone I am doing well. "I've made peace with it." Months later, I realized that I had never really gave myself time to mourn. I was so focused on looking strong on the outside that I really became weak on the inside. It was only after I finally admitted my pain— first to myself, then to others—that I truly began to heal. I had to embrace the fact that "It's Ok Not to Be OK!"

The ninth commandment warns against bearing false witness, and in grief, this applies to being honest about our emotions. Grief is one of the most difficult experiences a person can endure. It shakes our world, challenges our faith, and changes the way we see life. In the midst of sorrow, there is often a temptation to **lie about our grief**—to hide our pain, pretend we are okay, or suppress our emotions to make others more comfortable.

God calls us to truth, even in our sorrow. Jesus Himself wept openly when Lazarus died, showing that grief is not something to be hidden. If you are struggling, be honest with yourself. Speak your truth to those you trust. Seek out support rather than pretending everything is fine.

The Temptation to Lie About Grief

When someone asks, *"How are you doing?"* the natural response for many grieving people is:

- *"I'm fine."*
- *"I'm doing okay."*
- *"I'm getting through it."*

But in reality, they are hurting. They feel **empty, lost, confused, and broken.** They don't want to burden others with their emotions, so they put on a mask, pretending to be stronger than they really are.

Lying about grief often comes from a place of **fear or pride.**

- **Fear** that others won't understand.
- **Fear** of judgment.
- **Fear** of being seen as weak.
- **Pride** that says, *"I should be able to handle this on my own."*

But the truth is, **grief is not meant to be carried alone.** When we lie about our pain, we reject the very help and comfort that God has placed in our lives.

How Lying About Grief Hurts Us

Lying about our grief doesn't just affect the people around us—it **deepens our own suffering.**

1. Lying Keeps You Stuck in Pain

Healing requires **acknowledging** grief, not pretending it doesn't exist. When we suppress our emotions, we don't actually heal—we just push the pain deeper inside. But buried pain does not disappear. It builds up, often leading to anxiety, depression, or even physical health problems.

2. Lying Pushes Others Away

When we are dishonest about our grief, we **push away** the people who love us.

- Friends stop checking in because we act like we don't need support.
- Family members assume we are okay, when in reality, we are suffering in silence.
- Loved ones feel rejected when we refuse to open up.

The people in your life **want to help.** But if you continue to say you are fine, they may eventually believe you. **This leaves you feeling even more alone.**

3. Lying Prevents You from Receiving God's Comfort

God wants to bring healing, but **He cannot heal what we refuse to admit is broken.**

The Psalms are filled with **honest cries of grief**—David did not hide his sorrow from God. He wept, questioned, and cried out in pain. Then **God met him in that place of honesty.**

"How long, Lord? Will you forget me forever? How long will you hide your face from me? How long must I wrestle with my thoughts and day after day have sorrow in my heart?" **Psalm 13:1-2:**

David did not pretend to be okay—he was raw, open, and vulnerable with God. And because of his honesty, he received **comfort, strength, and renewal.**

You do not have to pretend in your prayers. **God already knows your heart.** The moment you are honest, healing begins.

Healing starts with honesty. When you acknowledge your grief, you allow yourself the space to work through it. Do not bear false witness against your own heart—tell the truth, and let healing begin.

Reflection:

Lying about grief does not protect you—it only prolongs the pain. Healing begins when you **are honest**—with yourself, with others, and with God.

Grief is heavy, but **you don't have to carry it alone.**

Instead of hiding your grief, choose honesty.

- When someone asks how you are doing, it's okay to say, *"I'm struggling today."*
- When you feel overwhelmed, it's okay to say, *"I need help."*
- When grief feels too heavy, it's okay to say, *"I don't know how to move forward."*

Application Assignment

- Have I been honest about my grief, or have I been pretending to be okay?
- Who in my life can I talk to about my emotions?
- How can I bring my real feelings to God in prayer?

X

The Tenth Commandment of Grief

Thou shall not covet another persons' Grief.

Exodus 20:17 -

"Thou shall not covet."

Thou Shall Not Covet Another Persons' Grief.

The Tenth Commandment of Grief
Thou Shall Not Covet Another Persons' Grief.
(Exodus 20:17 - "Thou shall not covet.")

Grief is deeply personal. No two people grieve the same way, and **there is no single "right way" to mourn.** However, one of the greatest struggles people face in grief is comparing their sorrow to others. Some wish they could be as "strong" as someone else, while others resent those who seem to move forward too quickly. This comparison leads to unnecessary pain, misunderstandings, and even resentment.

Just as God created each of us uniquely, **He also designed us to process grief differently.** The way someone mourns is shaped by their **circumstances, age, life experiences, personality, emotional resilience, and faith.** Instead of coveting—or judging—how someone else grieves, we must learn to honor the personal journey of every person. Your season of mourning may not look like someone else's, and **that is okay.**

Why Grieving Looks Different for Everyone

Many factors influence the way someone experiences and expresses grief.

1. Life Circumstances Shape Grief

The circumstances surrounding a loss can deeply impact how someone mourns.

- A person who loses a loved one after a long illness may grieve differently than someone who loses someone suddenly in an accident.
- A person who has lost multiple loved ones over time may

grieve differently than someone experiencing loss for the first time.

Grief does not follow a formula. **What looks like strength in one person may actually be deep internal sorrow. What looks like weakness in another may simply be an honest expression of pain.**

2. Age and Emotional Maturity Affect Grief

A child, a teenager, a young adult, and an elderly person will all grieve differently.

- A child may not fully understand the permanence of loss and may go between sadness and playfulness.
- A teenager may act out or withdraw, struggling to express emotions in words.
- An adult may carry the weight of responsibilities, suppressing grief to function in daily life.
- An elderly person may process grief through deep reflection and longing for reunion in eternity.

It is unfair to expect everyone to **grieve in the same way or on the same timeline.** We must offer patience, grace, and understanding.

3. Personal Loss History Affects Grief

A person who has **experienced multiple losses** may react differently than someone grieving for the first time.

- Someone who has been through **deep loss before** may seem "strong" because they have learned how to process pain.
- Someone who has **never experienced loss** may feel completely lost, overwhelmed, or even numb.

Grief is not a competition. **No one grieves "better" than someone else.** Each person must walk their own path toward healing.

4. Faith and Spiritual Maturity Influence Grief

A person's relationship with God can deeply impact the way they grieve.

- A strong believer may trust in God's plan and find peace more quickly.
- Someone struggling in their faith may feel abandoned, lost, or angry at God.
- A person with little spiritual foundation may feel hopeless, unsure of what happens after death.

Faith **does not erase pain,** but it does offer **a foundation for healing.** However, even the strongest believer struggles. We should never assume that a person's faith is weak just because their grief is overwhelming.

Grief is not meant to be compared—it is meant to be experienced, processed, and healed through God's grace. Trust your own journey and allow Him to guide you through it. Instead of **comparing** grief, we should **compassionately support one another.** God meets each of us in our unique grief. There is no need to compare—only to seek Him.

Loss changes everything. When something or someone you love is taken from you, it is natural to look around and notice what others still have. **A mother grieving the loss of her child may feel pain when she sees another mother holding her baby. A man who has lost his wife may ache when he watches couples celebrate anniversaries. A person who has lost a job may feel resentment toward those who still have financial stability.**

Grief makes us aware of what we no longer have, but **if we are not careful, it can also make us covet what others still do.**

While it is human to feel sorrow when we see reminders of our loss, **jealousy, resentment, and bitterness will only deepen the wound.** Instead of allowing grief to make us envious, we must learn to embrace gratitude, love, and healing—even when it feels difficult.

Do Not Hate Holidays and Celebrations Because of Your Loss

For those who are grieving, holidays can be painful reminders of what is missing. While others celebrate with family and friends, you may feel a deep ache, longing for the person who should still be here.

It is easy to **dread special days, avoid celebrations, and even grow to hate the holidays** that once brought joy.

- **Mother's Day, Father's Day, birthdays, anniversaries, Thanksgiving, Christmas, and other holidays** can feel like unbearable burdens rather than moments of joy. Its hard to think about the missing sit at the table.

- Seeing others celebrate **can make you feel isolated, as though the world is moving on without you.**

Embrace the People Who Try to Fill the Void

When someone you love is gone, no one else can **replace them.** However, God often sends people into our lives to **help carry the weight of grief.** The late rapper Tupac said this in his song You are Appreciated "Aint a women alive that can take my mama place". You may also feel like this however, God sees your loss and **He sends people into your life to help you heal.**

Sometimes, grief **makes us reject these people.** We push away love because **we feel like no one else can take their place.** Instead of rejecting love, **embrace the people who try to fill the void with kindness, companionship, and care.**

In Conclusion

Suffering a loss is one of the hardest things we will ever experience, but **God has promised that grief is not the end of our story.** The Bible reminds us in Revelation 21:4, *"He will wipe every tear from their eyes. There will be no more death, or mourning, or crying, or pain, for the old order of things has passed away."*

Until that day, we must grieve with hope. Until that day, we must grieve with hope. We must walk forward—not in comparison to others, but in the trust that **God is with us, carrying us through every moment of sorrow."** As we heal, we must remember that our lives are **still worth living, still worth loving, and still full of purpose.**

May we grieve with faith, may we love with endurance, and may we heal with the confidence that **we are never alone.**

Assignment Application:

- **Practice celebrating others.** The next time someone shares a joyful moment, congratulate them instead of withdrawing.

- **Reframe your perspective.** Instead of focusing on what you don't have, write a list of what you still do.

- **Choose healing.** Each day, remind yourself that your grief is yours to walk through—at your own pace, in your own way.

Thank You for Supporting

NATHAN E. AUSTIN
—— MINISTRIES ——

For Additional Books, Speaking Engagements or Workshops

You may contact us at:
954.977.7101
pastora@positioned2prosper.org
www.positioned2prosper.org/pastornathanaustin

1525 NW 7th Street
Pompano Beach FL. 33069

Nathan Eagle Austin/NEA Ministries-Facebook
Nathan.E.Austin -Instagram
@pastornea-Twitter

**PURCHASE
THE 10 COMMANDMENTS
OF LOVE**

www.ingramcontent.com/pod-product-compliance
Lightning Source LLC
Chambersburg PA
CBHW071010160426
43193CB00012B/1998